FINISHING LINE PRESS
www.finishinglinepress.com

AF472066

Summer Forgets to Wear a Petticoat

poems by

Mehnaz Sahibzada

Finishing Line Press
Georgetown, Kentucky

Summer Forgets to Wear a Petticoat

ISBN 978-1-944899-05-9 First Edition

ACKNOWLEDGMENTS

The following poems, sometimes in earlier drafts, have appeared in the following publications:

"Damsel Ghost" (and "Muse Noir") in the *Pacific Coast Poetry Series'* forthcoming anthology of Los Angeles Poets (2015)
"Muse Noir" appeared in *The 5-2 Crime Poetry Weekly*, June 2014
"Between the Hangers in *The Rattling Wall*, Issue 4, 2014
"The White Dress" in *The Rattling Wall*, Issue 4, 2014
"Neon Vulture" in *The Night Goes on All Night: Noir Inspired Poems*, 2011*
"China Silk Shoes" Mascara Literary Review, 2010*
"Hopeless Romantic" in *Strange Cargo*, 2010*
"A Room" in *South Asian Review*, Creative Writing Issue, Volume 31, Number 3, 2010*
*Published as "Mehnaz Turner"

In crafting this collection, I am indebted to the inspiration and guidance of numerous people, both personally and professionally: Erika Ayon, Tresha Haefner, Anna Journey, Donna Hilbert, Chris Kinnear, Suzanne Lummis, Michelle Meyering, Leslie Monsour, Afzal Sahibzada, Farhana Sahibzada, and Naureen Sahibzada. I am also grateful for the mentorship I received in Pen USA's Emerging Voices Fellowship program (2009); and the guidance I received through Pen's Mark Program (2011). This manuscript could not have been completed as it stands today without the assiduous support of these individuals and organizations.

Editor: Christen Kincaid
Cover Art: Debra Hughes, Shutterstock.com
Author Photo: Chris Kinnear
Cover Design: Elizabeth Maines

Printed in the USA on acid-free paper.
Order online: www.finishinglinepress.com
also available on amazon.com

Author inquiries and mail orders:
Finishing Line Press
P. O. Box 1626
Georgetown, Kentucky 40324
U. S. A.

Table of Contents

"There is too much tendency to attribute to God the evils that man does of his own free will."

—Agatha Christie, The Moving Finger

DAMSEL GHOST

Every city girl could use a boat.
And a lake. And an empty afternoon
to sail out west. Which is why

I put on the white dress, the one
I'd bought at an estate sale, grabbed
my childhood quilt, and brushed

my hair till it shook. I hung a lantern
on the prow and let the winds
lead the way. Nobody knew I was

fleeing. I'd tossed my cell away
in the laundry pile, my flip-flops
in the sink. No I wasn't drunk.

I didn't drink. But I'd been looking
at these pictures of swans all morning,
wishing I'd been born with a longer

neck. Someone who could freely
drift up the coast. Someone who
didn't live on cigarettes and toast.

But here I was, escaping the magic
monotony of my life. No one's wife,
no one's mother. Just a damsel ghost.

The trees hung gray. The sun
a shadowed eye blinking. The good
news was the boat drifted long,

didn't sink. And I felt tall and wild—
three candles lit. My breathing
slowed. I was miles from L.A. The day

was water, mountains, air, and I'd
escaped. No insight came, but this I knew:
Every city girl could use a boat. A white

dress and a lake. And an afternoon quilted
with golden thread, after a morning
in bed staring at photographs of swans.

GHAZAL FOR WINTER

Strong coffee—my liquid vice. Hot or cold.
Give me a hint of red spice. Hot or cold.

Ethiopia. Yemen. Sufi shrines.
I pay the fair market price. Hot or cold.

I'm a shy woman. Audacious. Bold.
Will you douse my drink with ice? Hot or cold.

Roasted, baked, or brewed—from Bombay to Rome.
Coffee house, School of the Wise. Hot or cold.

This Wine of Araby and your kisses—
the taste tempting and precise. Hot or cold.

Mehboob, I want to share a cup with you.
In a rainstorm would be nice. Hot or cold.

But this summer stretches to Malabar.
I call on sips for advice. Hot or cold.

In the winter, drinks taste sweeter—kisses.
The fog rolls in to entice. Hot or cold.

BETWEEN THE HANGERS

I stopped acting eighteen at thirty,
started wearing petticoats, baking cakes.
Began using words like irreversible
and certainly. Even spiritual slipped
into my vocabulary. I planted a garden
in my mouth and bought miniature dog
sculptures from a card shop downtown.
In the evenings, I'd read Jane Austen
novels while making dinner. The settings
on my car radio switched from classic rock
to classical. Sometimes, over lunch,
I'd trace people's auras, not worried
about being called the eccentric schoolgirl.
My clothes changed from dark to lavender.
Sundays, I saw God peering at me
between the closet hangers, sometimes
holding a tiny scroll. It might have been
a cigarette. Still I blinked hard when I
wasn't sure. God was certainly a non-smoker,
at worst an ex-smoker. Heaven, I imagined,
smelled like a river darkened by cloves.
But God was once eighteen too when
the hands are eager to clutch and choices
seem reversible. Is this why his visits were
more like lurks? These days the kind world
presses against the shadows in my mind,
and when I sit down for afternoon tea,
I cross my legs. I spend more time
in the kitchen now, slicing onions
and mincing garlic. I alphabetize my spices.
Often I see hints of sky above my stove.
The kitchen smells of mountain peaks,
but it's in my closet, where I store my shoes
and masks, that God calls on me in the dark.

VALENTINE'S CARD

for C.K.

You were surprised to see women
in the mariachi band—ordered more

tequila, guacamole dip. I said,
I should've studied Spanish in high school,

not French. You nodded, lit my
cigarette outside the restaurant. No

rain fell. Stars ornamented, dusty & dry,
above the drought-scented night on Reseda.

I tucked a rose behind my ear
because you asked me to. Your red shirt

made me think of Christmas. If I'd
worn flamenco heels, I would've danced

with you on the sidewalk. You laughed at my
tipsy wit, said, *You're shivering. Let's*

go home. I didn't protest. It was best
to leave my spinning thoughts alone. How

I was almost forty but still missed the sewn
navy comforter I slept under through my teens.

Never warm enough, it seemed. I thought
of the Valentine's card you gave me:

pink goldfish, glossy sheen. Nights like
this I quivered, a bubble eye in the breeze.

DETECTIVES IN THE SAMOSA SHOP

I ordered mint & tamarind—my nose in a book. Who had poisoned this country girl: the maid, an errant lover? Each paragraph kept me guessing.

A cryptic buzz in the restaurant, but I didn't notice the detectives until page sixty-four. The waitress placed a basket on my table, two servings of chutney.

But suddenly I wasn't hungry. Like a costume party, the faces perplexed. Columbo? Jane Marple? Was that Sherlock Holmes seated across Poirot?

I watched them dip & crunch, savor the cumin scent. Each seemed pensive, lost in some conundrum. Even the painted women in saris, red bangles at their wrists, appeared to puzzle over the room's conspicuous silence.

Soon Wallander drifted in as though Los Angeles were some Swedish pit stop. Then Nancy Drew in her plaid dress & headband, a girlish hurry in her step. I tried reading the next chapter, but now the restaurant presented a greater mystery.

One server turned up the Bollywood music. The door swung again: Sam Spade. Philip Marlowe. Even Father Brown, on the quest for Indian pastry. Each ordered the lunch special: two samosas, a cup of chai.

When Jessica Fletcher came by, I was ready to confess I wanted her autograph. I stopped myself from shouting "murder" to make her turn her head.

But this sudden convention of sleuths seemed oblivious that the dining room had become a synchronistic meeting place. It was April. The sun poured in through the windows, eager to illuminate mislaid clues.

THE WHITE DRESS

The psychics lied. He didn't call
on Tuesday. The whole weekend passed
and still the phone's silence predicted
nothing. I had clothes to wash. Sweaters
and scarves lay dormant across my bedroom
floor like petals off a vase. I called Hope
& Charity. Moonbeam and Lovelee too.
Each day, I surfed the website of clairvoyants
with a coke in my hand. The headlines
railed against sugar, still I clung
to the cold drops of sweetness, forgot
to load disks in the CD player, forgot
the climbing interest rates on my
credit card. Dialed and asked for
Shooting Star, waiting for the operator
to connect. *Monday*, she said. *Monday
your luck will change. And by April
you'll find cupid sitting on your left
shoulder again. You'll be writing odes
to breakfast, the resilience of men.*
But Monday came and went, and still
I forgot the CD's. The petals on my bedroom
floor grew wilder, mixed with the sudden
crunch of leaves, and I spent the evenings
hiding under a blanket, praying for a text
from God or someone else who sees
the past, present, and future simultaneously.
Someone pregnant with answers, who
might say, it's time to do your laundry
and put on the white dress. The one
you wore the night he pulled you close,
asked how often you read your horoscope.
The night you kissed as though winter
might never end, as though some hippie-
medium with flowers in her hair had seen
the moment years ago in a dream
on a calm-quiet night in Athens, Georgia.

MUSE NOIR

Every time I write, I sense his hand sliding
up my thigh. Blackening each metaphor, he hammers
my good-girl past until it shatters like a glass mug.

I can't shrug him away. One night in Lahore
when I was fifteen, he climbed beside me in bed,
fastened a palm around my wrist. It was the only

time I saw his face, the square brown chin
and espresso-stained grin, the cunning smile that
colonized my head. I said, *When I get back*

to California, I'll grind you up like a bean. But
he just waved a palm-sized cross and proposed.
I said yes, of course. Still he stood me up

for prom. I wore the ruby dress with the side
slit and waited on the porch. Waited and waited
until my thoughts took of their heels and like a corpse

stood still. For months he did not show. I spent
the evenings sketching black tulips, drinking coffee–
the café the one place he was likely to be–the air

prayer-whipped with the nuns who liked to visit,
play chess in the corner. There the lighting was
lunar. One night, reading a ghost story in the back,

my thoughts woke electric. I put on lipstick,
pressed it on even too. His hand gripped my neck.
The fear delicious, the joy rose up so fast,

I couldn't move. *If I stay*, he said,
you'll carry delusions, make mad like
Edgar Allen Poe. I told him I wasn't the kind

of girl who wanted a rose. He laughed at my quiver,
handed me a silver ring, something gothic. We
didn't kiss. It would have been uncouth

with the nuns watching. But the verdict
was in. My conscience mugged by a thief, I was
wife to spinning dark, to gunfire on the street.

REMNANTS

Astronomy depends on random conversations
in supermarkets. Ask any stargazer:

there is a need for plain communication.
Every syllable uttered in the routine vernacular

carries wind chimes of galaxy.
Still, the memories leap as I step

in line at checkout twelve. Across from me
the magazines speak in glossy whispers.

Stars airbrushed and suntanned.
Once the pages ignited childhood dreams.

But now I don't ask the bright
images to bring me constellations.

When the cashier says, credit or debit,
his words are a consolation. So much

we drift in staggers beyond our senses.
The night sky a silhouette of empty parks.

It's a blessing to be asked a manageable question,
to speak the answer without a planet

weighing down the tongue. The stars
watching from above catch remnants

of their sparks in our daily exchanges.
As scientists, focusing their telescopes,

stand on the shoulders of functional speech
to forge pathways to the unexplained.

AGATHA CHRISTIE GETS BUTTERFLIES

She arrived before he did.
Picked at the peanuts.
The dating guide had said,
No phones. She slipped
her cell into a mini-clutch.
The painting on the wall swayed,
a red herring. The gastro pub
was all whispers. She told
the waitress, *Ginger beer.*
Show him you're fun,
the book had said.
Why hadn't she chosen
the blue dress? In white,
she shook like a lampshade.
He arrived before Tuesday.
His T-shirt read,
Only in Saudi Arabia.
But he'd never left Los Angeles.
Travel interested him
less than detective novels.
According to the website,
they were a 96% match.
She took a swig of her beer,
remembering the book.
The gist had been, *Lie.*
Later his hand slipped
over hers, so she spilled her drink.
He went to the restroom,
brought back napkins.
Make him your hero,
the book had said. \
For dinner they ate slices
of Hawaiian pizza. She took
small bites, as if to say,
I used to be a dancer.
His story about a missing
writer puzzled her. She laughed
to make him feel like he'd traveled.
Then a tickle in her throat.
Was she allergic to peanuts?
He handed her a glass of water.
Shivering, she blinked like
a suspect. The plot was hazy now,
but suddenly, butterflies.

NEON VULTURES

Summer in Los Angeles, and the city's covered
my shoulders in mosquito bites. The air's so thick

I could cut up slices to refrigerate. My mood's
not deliberate. Every time I step out of my apartment,

someone hands me a shot glass. Sometimes I wanna
say, *Do I look like a broad who needs to lighten up?*

I wear fishnets under my jeans. On Monday mornings,
the cars wheel heavily down the freeway's length.

I blink back the glances of predators. Like a newspaper
headline, my hopes reek wrath. And in downtown

or Venice, no matter how much red I wear, I'm a picture
cropped in gray and black. Touch my neck. You'll find

it's charged with light. Still, mosquitoes slip through
the cracks, find a way to bite into my wine-rich skin.

Drunk and dizzy on blood, they travel back down
Sunset, past the bars and taco stands, to the Laundromat

on Vermont, where insomniacs count quarters after
midnight. My fortune-teller says, *This place feeds*

on a woman's flesh. Burn your novels. Drink tequila.
Streak your hair orange. When people ask you what

you do, say, 'I just try to mesh'. The truth is, the city
waits for the right moment to knock you up before

it runs you over. Even the cops and gangsters fall prey
to chance. If you're lucky, you'll miss the neon vultures

trying to hook you in at every street corner. Summer
doesn't end for months. The sun's a crab scuttling

across the shores of Malibu, watching thieves
and pickpockets surf the streets. If you've got the guts,

score a gun. These hardboiled days, luck can't be
bought for a few dimes at the thrift store on Vineland.

GLOVES

I live in the United States
of poetry, in the quest
to be united with the white graffiti
past my terrorist thoughts.
On caffeinated Mondays,
I state my opinion without poetry.
At work formulate intuitions,
prepositions. Once in a meditation class,
over and under, above and beyond
I went. I saw my heart was in a state
of neglect, felt united with a photograph
I once saw of a supernova
in a textbook. This sensation expanded
into poetry. See, every word we've
ever heard lives tucked in the spine.
Every assault and tenderness,
every trick of the tongue. United
they live quashed in a state of fury,
and this fury is poetry
because the silence drifts
under and behind, below and around
each thought. Because the heart
is a supernova in the galaxy of each body.
Because driving the freeway
during rush hour traffic
I am dubious about gloves,
how in winter wearing them serves
practical purposes, but they're itchy
and dark. The gloves tick like a bomb
on my hands and soon
I have to take them off to feel the frost,
the fog on my fingertips.
The heart too needs to breathe
and the body is a glove.
And the two live in a state nearsighted,
and the distance between them
is poetry. The quest, to be united.
At night I lie in bed, think,
Girl, you're an aging star.
Still I get my eyebrows waxed
and honk at drivers who cut me off.
Busy lunches, my fork stabs lettuce,
and cucumber slices.
Tomatoes. Celery stalks.

CLASSIC

We kissed and Frankenstein. I wore the gold necklace with the elephant pendant. We kissed and Madame Bovary. The elephant jingle-jangled against my neck. It was 2am, and LAX had never looked so historical. You held my hand, and I held A Tale of Two Cities. You said, *That elephant's a sun against your dark skin.*

I grinned to Wuthering Heights. You wanted to know if the pendant was a gift. I knew what you were really asking. My ex was an entomologist. Had he been the one, it would have been a cockroach or a beetle. Not this matriarchal mammal, not this gold miniature of hefty thighs.

We embraced in Pride and Prejudice. My fears and Dracula. You said, *it's a sin to call collect.* I said, *It's a sin to shoot an elephant.* Our future was born in 1984. Our world, a Cannery Row of fisherman. It was 2:04, and LAX had never looked so intellectual. You asked me if you could keep the necklace while I was away—the little gold trunk and tusks and teeth.

But I would be the one boarding and departing, hovering over The Good Earth. I needed a totem. You said, *Our love is the totem.* I opened my shoulder bag and handed you a slice of bread. Your eyes misted over, and you poked the tip of your chin with an index finger, dropped the slice back inside my bag.

I said, *I'll chop off my hand, but I'm holding on to the elephant.* It was 2:07, and LAX had never looked so metaphorical. *I really need to get in line*, I said. But you surprised me by reaching for my neck. A tug, a pull, an unhesitating yank. Then the necklace in your grip. My mouth flew open.

This elephant's a classic, you said. *And I'm man enough to wear it.* I stood still—stunned. Handed you my carry-on bag. *You fly then*, I said. *You board the god damn plane. You speak at that conference in Chicago. You write the next great American dissertation. I'm going to the zoo.* I hailed a taxi and didn't look back.

That morning, gazing at a zebra, I decided losing the elephant pendant had been my karma. I'd probably been a hunter in some previous life. You'd probably flown to India to meet your match. The truth was I'd bought the elephant to remind myself I was just an animal with veins. LAX was eminently nonsensical. Life seesawed between War and Peace.

IF I WROTE A MYSTERY NOVEL

I'd make the detective a lexicographer, word-travelled
and prone to fits of chatter, to interrogating questions like,

What's the matter with this world? He'd be serpent-like
and prim, addicted to sunsets, how watching them made him

believe in God. The victim would be a broad who liked
to fuss and meddle, who'd made love to half the town,

and in her see-through gown could be spotted shopping
for lentils at the market. She'd make an obvious target.

And the villain, to be sure, would have a sketch of humor.
Slipping on loafers, he might noose her or gag her

in his mid-town loft and from here the plot would emerge.
I know it's wrong to kill and even when I've stepped

on a spider crawling across my kitchen floor in winter,
I've felt like a jealous spinster for quashing hope. So why

this obsession with thinking up wrong? I should pen a story
about fairies or unicorns. Once, on a train ride to Seville,

I sat near the window transfixed by the hills, the Spanish
Clouds—wanting, somehow, to make my mind work like

the labyrinth streets of Cordoba. At twenty-two I had hopes
of unraveling mysteries, but the world, since then has rarely

whispered answers to me. It shouts its catcalls and invectives,
and when I'm down, slurs, *order another drink*. My mind's

a shot glass in a sink, and that train ride from years ago
seems a dream I slept through once on a bus ride to the library.

Maybe it's not answers I've been after, but to enter the threat
of an imminent disaster—to touch a blade. Sometimes

I want to live in black and white, in the courtyard of noir,
imagining I have the power to masquerade as moonlight.

To channel the detective lexicographer crafting & compiling.
Words noosed, gagged, kidnapped. Each part of speech, suspect.

HOPELESS ROMANTIC

I load the dishwasher
as though twelve Buddhist monks
are sitting *zazen*[1] in my living room.
Out the shaded window,
a sparrow sings hymns to the sunlight.
Her whistling reminds me the rays
spill to the ground like weightless trophies,
but I'm not ready to look.
Tonight, I think, I'll stand near the vase
of tulips to mix the *chapathi* [2] dough,
shape odes with my fingers. I'll teach
my worries about irony, draw back
the blinds to reveal the purgatory
of what matters. It's an obligation,
really, to keep the blinds open
sometimes. To gaze up at the stars
and recognize the mind's cadence
in the distance between stars. To load
each dish so excellently every clang
betrays the chivalry of silence.

[1]In meditation pose.
[2]Flat unleavened bread.

THE DETECTIVE WHO SPOKE URDU

found me on the beach.
He arrived in a dream. We stood in the heat

and a woman, dressed
in a glitter gown, sang the Blues by the waves.

The sun, darker than a thumb
print, blinked on a page of sky. And the detective—

an Englishman—spoke in Urdu,
(a surprise) said: *Do you have an alibi?*

But the truth I couldn't tell him.
That I'd spent my life chasing mysteries,

dreamt of marrying a sleuth.
When I was sixteen, I watched *Columbo*

every week, but he never ate
samosas, drank *chai.* Still, he was the kind of guy

who made me blush. This beach
was neither the Pacific nor the Indian. Not

the Black nor the Caspian. It bore
no original name. I found it in the American noir

of my subconscious, which
was a cacophony of waves, the woman's

sonorous voice. The sun
so slick it fired like a gun. The detective

who spoke Urdu stood
waiting for me to speak. But I couldn't talk,

my knees weak. Shy, even
in my dreams. I trembled like the waves.

IRONING A DRESS

Big tired book, *Jane Eyre.* Heavy
in my hands. Twenty-two lines
to describe a desk lamp. Must we really
hear each minute detail? And why so many
big words, fancy words, sentences that take
the scenic route to their period? Endless details
on sewing and school lunches and tutoring
sessions in French. And Mr. Rochester,
that curmudgeon, must he really occupy
so many paragraphs? The pace alternating
between slow and emphatically slow. I turn
your pages, *Jane Eyre,* and seasons change
in my city, and still the protagonist is ironing
a dress. But my grandmother kept you
on her bedside table. My mother handed me
your story when I was thirteen, said,
Here, read this. Every woman should.
So to keep warm I travel your pages
again and again. Sometimes the disciplined
teacher, others the madwoman in the attic.

A MONK MIGHT FIND ME SUPERFICIAL

My friend, the editor, was dating a memoirist.
He had written boldly about his liquor cabinet,
spotting hummingbirds just south of Tucson.
Over a salad lunch she spoke on and on
about their dates, the work of fate
in bringing them together, their post-sex talks.
Watching her pepper the bowl of lettuce in front
of her, I thought of the yellow walls of my
living room, which needed a fresh coat of paint.
I thought of high school and college, and how
little I used my voice. My teen years and still,
I could be passive as a trail of yarn. I asked
questions, rarely answered them, and the whole
world seemed to be rushing on, moving forward,
while the destination was lost on me, and I
listened to the same songs. But the love
poured out when I kissed a man, and years ago
while manicuring my nails red in a Laundromat,
I thought I was destined for the scarlet life.
I went clothes shopping more deliberately from
then on and decided my closet wasn't just a
functional space but an argument being formed,
each hanging garment, a line of evidence. *Every
time we coordinate an outfit*, I told my sister once,
we are entering the debate. And though a monk
might find me superficial, I would only agree
on my green pump days. Most weeks I shrine
my walk in boot cut jeans. I listen to Paul
Simon. I dress to succeed at the post office.

A RED DRESS

I've never lied while holding a rose, but once
I did while holding a tulip. I was in London,

boarding a train to Edinburgh, my thoughts
braided with strands of *Gandhi* and *Foucault.*

I had been wondering about the benefits
of selfishness. Above me the light shimmered

maudlin prophecies. I wanted a French kiss
with someone I didn't know—an improvisational

show, a sudden skit. I wore a red dress that
could have been stitched by the hands of some

church-going whore, or maybe a deaf-mute
spinster whose hands knew no speed but slow.

I could read a magazine on my journey to kill
time. How many times had I killed an hour just

hanging low, doing some inconsequential thing?
That day, however, I held a yellow tulip. Above me,

the light wore ballet slippers. Inside the train,
I prayed for a fine seat-mate, a handsome beau.

But an old woman sat down to my right
in Compartment D, offered me a spoon of jam,

a cup of tea. She shared philosophies on the changing
world. I'd spent a thousand dollars on an airline

ticket to experiment. And here I was listening to some
grandma's lament. So when she asked where I was

headed, I simply said: *To a brothel, ma'am, to find
some work*. She seemed to lean away then, stare

out the window at the passing moths. As for me,
I had no room for wise regret. At twenty-two, I treated

life like a Bollywood film-set. The words had floated out.
I'd made a foe. I would sleep and sleep till Edinburgh.

SUMMER FORGETS TO WEAR A PETTICOAT

I bought the straw hat with black ribbon, thinking
about Sherlock Holmes. Sometimes I wear

it on walks around the neighborhood.
The buildings & vacant schools don't resemble

Baker Street. In my twenties, I drank a lot of tea:
PG Tips—a dash of milk, a spoonful of sugar.

Why do habits form then suddenly vanish? Sometimes
marriages—whole cities disappear. Last week

a flash of lightening struck Venice Beach. Even summer
forgets to wear a petticoat when clouds appear.

It's easier to swim and surf without a shield. I never
took a statistics course, but on evening walks

I probe the data of my life. In the absence of green,
clues & hints remain unseen, flare on impulse.

THE MISUNDERSTOOD ARE SELDOM EXTROVERTED

It was the era when shy people spoke
out like activists on the march.

Enumerated the benefits of introversion:
depth & sensitivity. Profundity. Wisdom.

Once I had a party where I invited No One.
I made biryani listening to Bach. I had

recently read a post about saffron which
helped me understand the predicament

of the quietly bold. It's sublime to spend
your evenings planning a murder. The

imagination is a weapon. I used a chef's knife
to cube the chicken, mince the garlic. Wore

a black dress with a floral hem. Danced
after dinner with the blinds closed. I took

no pictures to post on the web. Scooped
daydreams for dessert at this solo celebration.

A POEM THAT WANTS TO BE A PASTRY

In the department store dressing room,
I decide to make a career change.

Pink dress, green dress—neither one
seems brave enough. I hail a taxi,

tell the driver, *Head west.* At the
police station, the inspector taps

his watch as I confess: *Pink dress,*
green dress—neither one seemed

brave enough. But no smile
beneath the mustache. *If you're*

bored, Ma'am, write a novel. A job
like this will make a tourist faint.

Later in the abyss of my afternoon,
I stop for baklava. Eat the pistachio filled

pastry on my balcony with a cup of tea.
At 6:22 I tell the spider crawling across

a patio chair that he will never be
a butterfly. But the arachnid grows

wings bluer than the sky. Poses,
as if to say, I'm headed for the moon.

A POEM THAT WENT WINE TASTING

Vacations are like rose petals in a soup,
sweet and exotic. On the couch I think of Napa.

Vashon Island. Joshua Tree. I like to kiss you
wearing leg warmers, after I've sipped tea.

It doesn't have to be raining—there need not be
music playing. But in solitude, I wonder about

priests who travel to penitentiaries—do they find
their work romantic? Once I saw a picture

of a serial killer & imagined him holding a rose.
For a moment, I was less afraid. I like to kiss you

wearing leg warmers, after I've sipped tea.
It doesn't have to be raining—there need not

be music playing. But if you've ever twirled around
a pole while gazing in a mirror, then you know

the body is a weapon. The imagination, its muse.
When I'm with you I forget there are sociopaths

among us. I talk of wine tasting at Madrigal.
The board of cheeses, our Moroccan guide.

A POEM THAT WANTS TO BE A SPICE IN THE CUPBOARD

I never wanted
to be a chef—
but now I leave
footprints
on the kitchen floor,
fingerprints
savory & sweet.
I've learned eight lemons
yield a cup of juice.
I surf the web
reading recipes like poems.
Name my plants:
Paprika, Turmeric.
When people ask me
about God, I tell them
about my pantry.
Tiny cupboard
in a tiny space,
but I don't need more.
The cakes
come out the oven
as though
baked in a rich man's home.
I marinate chicken
& lamb chops.
Roast potatoes,
season asparagus.
When people
ask me where
I pray, I don't say the mosque.
Little white kitchen, I say.
Sticky poetry books
stained with last night's
meal.
I cook to feel.
French music, my gourmand.
A cup of coffee,
my sous-chef.

BITTER WATER

Choco-loca-lit. Noir kiss. Dark rum. Coarse peppermint. Milk slick, corporate trimmed. Wine savored, wicked excellence. Choco-drink. Liquid bliss. Shot glass, pure silk. Orange-flavored, orange-tinged. Paki skin, breath, brown gin. Ritually, I sip & sip. Blood lips, choco-stained. Interrogate me, intoxicate. My passport a choco-page. This country, a choco-stage. Choco-people cohabitate. Dipping, dipping, anticipate. Belgian. Milky Swiss. I taste the Aztec, *xocolatl* [1]. Bitter water, bitter war. Bitter headlines, bitter dark. Bitter coffee I drink to start. Bitter coffee, to start my day. The night is white with choco-stars. Choco-moon and choco-light. A choco-mosque, a news headline. Choco-lanes in choco-towns. Choco-thieves, choco-found. I sip & sip. My hands bleed brown. In Montezuma's grip, the past a crown. A seat of spark, a crystal sound. Choco-noble, masculine. The Spanish drank their choco dark. Men bought prostitutes with cocoa pods. They drank till drunk, corrupt, unfeminine & sold their slaves for choco-sin.

[1]Chocolate

A ROOM

I wasn't born blond or freckled,
wanting skin like milk
saying, *Just send me a text*
if you wanna kiss. I wasn't
born wearing lip gloss or loving
boys who wore their hair
to their ears, said, *Dude, I'm*
jonesing for some mac and cheese,
wore T-shirts stained with
last night's spaghetti, clutched
their iPhones like my father held
his Qu'ran on my fourteenth birthday
saying, *Only touch this book*
after you've washed your tongue.
I wasn't born with a stethoscope
for a brain, a mind speaking science.
Not in a library near a fish tank,
nor on a beach breathing sea water,
Jamaican blue. I had no words,
no stories in my mold. Bathed
in my mother's scent, I fell
into the arms of a man in a white
coat and lay in a room in Lahore
where Dada[1] whispered Muslim prayers
in my ears, sprinkled me with gold.

[1]My paternal grandfather

REHAB CENTER FOR GOD ADDICTION

The sufferers came day after day lugging
their drug free suitcases, fanning themselves

with new science books. No Gods Exist,
the sign read. And there came random searches

for bibles and prayer mats, crosses and sacred beads.
Any sign of worship, and they kicked you out.

Reading scripture's a waste, they said. An addiction
like meth. Snort these lines quick, and you'll end up

a murderer. Each patient was branded "atheist",
and therapists led group talks where people cried

over years of blind dependence, obsession
with priests. Everything's random, the doctor

said. Our bodies made from stardust. Isn't this
miracle enough? Abortion clinics get defamed

by the addicted. Fundamentalism circles the globe.
But the days stretched long at rehab, and people

struggled with the dizzying sense of freedom.
Mealtimes triggered some to press palms together,

and for this they locked you in a room to watch
documentaries about the Taliban, the Crusades.

Our bodies are water and dust, the doctor said. God
worship's a disease. There's no proof of a creator's hand.

Everyone must agree. Still it was acceptable to sit
by the koi pond at dusk and stare up at the moon, even

read your horoscope. Fine to write a song that praised
the mystery of the galaxy & sprang from nothingness.

UNDER THE STARS IN SAUDI ARABIA

Jeddah, Mecca, Taif. In every city, the desert
smelled of violets. Weekends, we ate French fries
on the beach, watched veiled women charge

into the Red Sea. My sister and I built sand castles
with golden domes , called each other "booger"
and "butt head" over plastic toy telephones. Our

parents always drove to the coast at night when
the stars blinked Arabic, the dunes shadowed
and desolate. I often gazed up at the sky, stories

of flying carpets and silver wands behind my eyes.
I was seven–knew no poems, no poets then, except
the spoken verses of the Quran, which were sung

at the Kaba[1] in voices rich as henna. Claimed
with tongues that kissed each word. Something
in me stirred amid those high mosque walls. I'd

listen to the call for prayer with my head tilted up
as though the sounds funneled out some cloud:
ethereal, loud. I'd listen with eyes closed, my head

draped in a purple scarf, thinking neither about hair
nor covering yet, but the arresting tide of words
rising, falling–calling in a language I didn't

understand but felt like a hand brushing the ear.
Just hearing the holy suras[2] made me feel wiser,
older. Those weekends we drifted between towns,

I never worried about disloyalty. The three years
we lived in Saudi, I never inked a line of simile. Yet
on Saturday nights, I mouthed Arabic recitations

with my lips–carried Mecca in the grip of my memory.
Under the stars, I wrote in the sand with my feet,
ate kabobs salted with splashes of the Red Sea.

[1]A building located inside a mosque in Mecca; considered the holiest place for Muslims.
[2]Chapters of the Quran.

SUMMER HAGIOGRAPHY

I wouldn't say I drank too much coffee. I spent
the afternoon searching for recipes on the web.

Sauced the chicken thighs with mustard & vinegar—
a pinch of smoked paprika. The whole apartment

smelled of Jamaica, of blue waters spiced with white
rum. I made the bed while the chicken marinated

in the fridge. I wouldn't say I drank too much coffee.
The phone rang twice, but the caller ID blinked

unknown number. I read twenty pages of a book,
listened to my neighbor playing his piano. Earlier

at the grocery, I'd wandered the aisles in search
of Dijon. So many interpretations—yellow, black,

and brown. Seeds and pastes. Coarsely ground
& powdered. The Romans used it first, sweetened

it with honey. Now we pair it with mayonnaise,
spread it on cold meats. Antibacterial, my mother says.

The Greeks claimed it cured scorpion stings. In India,
families sprinkled seeds along their front door to ward

off evil spirits. The cup was balmy & warm. I wouldn't
say I drank too much coffee. I peered into the pulse

of the sunny afternoon. Walked a block to dance class.
Painted my nails a shade of gold that made me think

of Cleopatra. Later you came home to a kitchen that
swayed like an altar. I savored the lingering taste

of brew, thought of making another. But we ate the
baked chicken with potatoes, sliced avocado for the salad.

The skin so crisp, it penned a hagiography on the tongue.
Dusk settled in to hints of mustard, sips of water.

ON READING AN AGATHA CHRISTIE MYSTERY IN BED

Three hundred pages and counting,
I sit under covers on my California
king, climbing out of my life
and into the blood-tinged question
marks along the English moors.
I shadow the detective, my hands
waving teacups behind his trench coat.
What twists lurk there, just past
the hills, near the King's Head pub?
Off the pages of a mystery novel,
the world's this echo of grass
and breath. Look now closely at these
rain-splashed footprints, maybe size
nine and a half. Later in Oxford more
clues may emerge. Even god, selfless
as a cow's udder, might squeeze us
a drop from his Eden of answers.

CHINA-SILK SHOES

I womaned my way into fourteen pairs in the rack.
Three more in the coat closet and four under my bed.

My lover hums the math, skims a puzzled look over
my feet. His favorites include the red sneakers and

flamenco heels. *Men are simple*, he says with a shake
of his head, as if complexity were a tarot deck.

And I wave through the twin response: part zen
teacher, part succubus. How can I explain that city

women live in the clickity-click of their imaginations.
The sidewalk's a runway, a yellow carpet spilling

into countries of leaf. How can I explain, when there
are the other days I wish I could pivot barefoot

through the weeks. But my soles would grow restless.
Nothing like a leather strap over each ankle to make

the dinner wine taste like meat. It's not just a pair
of shoes. It's that weeping woman in Picasso's oil

on canvas, getting up and stepping out. She gives her
hips a purposeful shake. *I'm headed crimson*, she says,

reaching into a kitchen bowl to grab a handful of cherries,
before she puts on her china-silk shoes and colors free.

Mehnaz Sahibzada was born in Pakistan and raised in Los Angeles. She holds an M.A. in Religious Studies from UC Santa Barbara, and she is a 2009 PEN USA Emerging Voices Fellow in Poetry. Her short story, "The Alphabet Workbook", appeared in the August 2010 issue of *Ellery Queen Mystery Magazine.* Her poetry chapbook, *Tongue-Tied: A Memoir in Poems*, was published in 2012 by Finishing Line Press. Her work has appeared in numerous publications, such as *Asia Writes, The Rattling Wall,* and *Pedestal Magazine.* A high school English teacher, she lives in southern California. To learn more about Mehnaz, visit her website at www.mehnazsahibzada.com

www.ingramcontent.com/pod-product-compliance
Ingram Content Group UK Ltd.
Pitfield, Milton Keynes, MK11 3LW, UK
UKHW042011190726
13854UKWH00005B/2240